Retire Ready

4 Lessons to Save Your Retirement Plan

Kyle Hammerschmidt

Retire Ready

Independently Published

Copyright © 2021, Kyle Hammerschmidt

Published in the United States of America

210405-01837.3.1

ISBN: 9798404534238

For more information on 90-Minute Books including finding out how you can publish your own book, visit 90minutebooks.com or call (863) 318-0464

relationship between the reader and the author or his firm.

Although great effort has been expended to ensure that only the most meaningful resources are referenced in these pages, the author does not endorse, guarantee, or warranty the accuracy reliability, or thoroughness of any referenced information, product, or service. Any opinions, advice, statements, services, offers, or other information or content expressed or made available by third parties are those of the author(s) or publisher(s) alone. References to other sources of information does not constitute a referral, endorsement, or recommendation of any product or service. The existence of any particular reference is simply intended to imply potential interest to the reader.

The views expressed herein are exclusively those of the author and do not represent the views of any other person or any organization with which the author is, or may be associated.

Here's What's Inside...

Beyond the Fine Print

Before investing any time reading through this book, let's take a look at who this book is intended for. Any time personal finance is being discussed, you must understand what you are listening to, or reading could have absolutely nothing to do with your financial situation.

I should probably begin by saying who this book is not for. First, if you are a professional financial procrastinator, this book is not for you. I'll get around to it eventually. Time is the most valuable asset, and taking action gives you better control. Before you even consider implementing or executing any recommendations or ideas outlined in this book, please consult a professional advisor. Next, if you are looking for the next hot stock, cryptocurrency, or ways to double your money in just five years, this book is not for you. What is the best investing strategy? There isn't one!

Everyone's financial situation is different. So technically, there isn't one right answer. It depends on personal factors: your income, risk tolerance, time horizon "when you need the money", current assets, and future financial goals.

I decided to invest some of my time into this book because I keep hearing the same things over and over again from pre-retirees and baby boomers. This book is for anyone whose current retirement plan consists of a stack of statements, a diversified pie chart, some magical savings number to hit, plus a Social Security statement. This book is also for anyone who is genuinely interested in getting the critical facts to make decisions in their own best interest. Sometimes logic is not enough, and we must go against conventional wisdom to accomplish our short and long-term goals.

Lastly, this book is best for anyone looking to invest time into their retirement planning. Sadly, a majority of baby boomers or pre-retirees will spend more time researching a $300 grill than why they own certain funds or stocks.

If you are concerned about taxes possibly going up, markets crashing up and down in retirement, when to claim Social Security around retirement accounts, and what order to withdraw your accounts from, then keep reading!

Introduction

One of the biggest problems baby boomers and pre-retirees face is finding the critical facts to make educated decisions regarding their retirement years. There are so many confusing avenues for finding "retirement information," including TV, online articles, radio, social media, and maybe even worse of all, the financial industry.

If there were a missing piece of information costing you money now or could potentially cost you significantly more money in the future, when would you want to find out about it?

What I have found over the years is that individuals 50 and up are not properly prepared when it comes to tax efficiency in retirement. They are not actively considering the major role the tax system plays in their retirement. The current plan they have, more times than not, is a tax time bomb, especially for a married couple. Another issue is the lack of a true investment philosophy behind the plan. Almost every time

I sit down with a household for the first time, their portfolio and philosophy are what I call "naked investing."

Their current asset allocations do not consider the money cycle and sequence of returns risk. The diversified pie chart and magic savings number do not mitigate market risk, interest rate risk and carry either not enough growth or too much unnecessary risk. Both instances can lead to premature depletion of savings! Another common problem is being able to understand the order of withdrawals. What accounts, what amounts, what income sources should be used first or in conjunction with each other to achieve tax efficiency now and later?

Last, the biggest problem is understanding that you are giving something up to gain something in return for every decision you make. Pre-retirees cannot take the approach that it is a linear process, and once you hit some magic number, it will all be fine! It is important to come to an understanding that pre-retirement and ongoing retirement needs to be more comprehensive. You need to have an income plan and understand desired cash flow and what math says is best for when to claim Social Security. If you have large 401(k)s and IRAs, the math might say to delay claiming to allow you to defuse your tax time bomb. There are too many tax tactics to cover in this book, but we will go over the most pressing ones to give you an idea of what's at stake.

My hope is, by reading this book, you are encouraged to challenge your thinking and expand your retirement planning. Some of you who read this will only get one or two golden nuggets out of it, but it will be like drinking from a fire hose for others. The goal is to inspire pre-retirees to invest more time and effort, so you can uncover the critical facts before making a decision that could impact your retirement outcome. The biggest reduction to your income in retirement could be from the decisions you make or do not make. In some instances, this could mean just a couple thousand dollars of difference or hundreds of thousands of income received and taxes in retirement paid.

My education-based approach primarily comes from the mindset that I want to teach you how to avoid the critical mistakes I see pre-retirees making, so you can *Retire Ready*; for enjoyment, relaxation, and time to do what YOU want to do.

Here's to Retiring Ready!

Kyle

Lesson One
The New Reality

Chapter One
Following the Herd

Traditional retirement planning is the pre-retiree or the baby boomer going through their working years, saving and saving, paying off debt, and raising a family. Typically, their avenue of saving for retirement is all chunked away in tax-deferred accounts, maybe an employer plan, an IRA, and anything like that.

That was very popular in the eighties and nineties, the early two-thousands, and up to today. Traditional retirement is a stack of statements with a diversified portfolio and aiming for this magic number of what you need to have saved to retire. Then, typically, you're going to claim your Social Security and use that magic number to replace your working income. In most cases, conventional wisdom is to take Social Security upon retirement or at Full Retirement Age plus a certain withdrawal percentage to make ends meet. That's why I look at a different approach, what we call a

21st-century approach. That's more where you're doing the comprehensive planning.

Following the Herd vs. Comprehensive Planning

Take a more comprehensive approach. Instead of focusing all on stock and fund picking, we're looking at your investments and making sure you're also factoring in taxes in retirement, the order of withdrawals "Income Planning", and Social Security strategies into retirement. The value of taking a more comprehensive approach is to make better investment decisions based on the time horizon for the income needed, to potentially lower your long-term taxes in retirement bill, and try to create extra income with assets already saved today. I explain how this all works together to ensure your retirement plan is as efficient as possible.

Certain things will happen over the next 30 years out of your control, and this way, you're properly prepared for when they do happen. Many things are going on right now with record low-interest rates, record-high stock markets, national debt, and a lot of money for pre-retirees chunked away in tax-deferred accounts. I don't think that the traditional planning approach is a bad way of going about it. With a little bit of education, you'll start to make decisions in your best interest and coordinate decisions when it comes to taxes in retirement, income planning, and your investments.

There's a common mentality that, "I've been using my 401(k) for 25 years, so I might as well keep doing the same thing before and into retirement." Let me tell you why you may or may not want to move forward with that mindset.

It's a transition. You're playing a new game. In the first phase, you're in accumulation. For most pre-retirees, income is in the fashion of dollar-cost averaging into the retirement account every two weeks with your own contributions plus the company's match. The biggest asset you have on your side is TIME, so you can make mistakes or wait for the markets to recover over time. One of the advantages of dollar-cost averaging is it allows you to buy low and high as the markets cycle through your accumulation phase. As you approach retirement or the preservation phase, where you're near retirement, or you're going to go into retirement and distribution, it's a whole new ball game.

Now you're going to be doing reverse dollar-cost averaging over your retirement years. What this means for most of you is very simple; selling high and selling low. This could lead to emotional decision-making not in your best interest now and in retirement. Hence, this is why every pre-retiree needs a comprehensive approach to retirement that uses a bucketing system for investing, a taxes in retirement plan to create tax-efficient income, and an income plan to maximize Social Security and address the order of withdrawals. You now lose the most valuable asset, TIME. We all know markets go up over time as long as you stay invested and make periodic contributions. Unfortunately, you or no one else has a crystal ball to what the first ten years of returns will be like for you in retirement. You're going to be relying on the money you saved over your working years to supplement a portion of your retirement income. Mistakes and setbacks are harder to come back from at that point, whether it's a tax event or a market correction, or anything like that. It's a way harder ball game than what you've been doing the last 30 years. To assume what worked before is going to keep on working may or may not be true.

The Problem with Not Transitioning

With traditional retirement planning, something you could be experiencing is maybe your plan consists of a stack of statements and a diversified pie chart. You're going to be leaning heavily on the stock market and its performance for you to be able to hit your retirement income goals. You could possibly be leaving extra tax dollars on the table by overpaying on Social Security tax or pulling too much out of an IRA at a certain point.

That's a very common experience you could have if you're going to go about it the cookie-cutter way. Again, that could work, but you might not have a plan for the sequence of returns risk. What happens if, in the first five years of your retirement, the market's not doing what you plan on it doing? Do you have a plan for that? Do you have your money invested based upon the time horizon of when you're going to need it? Are you able to execute your Social Security plan that allowed you to gain an additional $10,000 of provisional income every year in retirement? Do you have a plan in place for the order of withdrawals on your accounts? What accounts should be used first or in combination to achieve tax efficiency? Do you understand how IRA's and 401k's could cause your Social Security to be more taxable? Are you prepared for future tax hikes?

If you go about it with a comprehensive approach, you've properly positioned yourself for different outcomes to happen, where you can still come out at the end okay.

Joe and Sally's Story

I have a married couple we'll call Joe and Sally. Let's say they're in their early sixties. Both were great savers through their working years. They raised their family. They got them through college, and now they're empty nesters. A majority of the retirement funds were chunked away in tax-deferred accounts, the traditional way of going about it. They had next to no debt, and basically, their primary goal was to make sure that they saved enough to live on to maintain their current lifestyle.

Again, most of their saving was done through their current and former employer plans. They had a small percentage in their brokerage account at a wirehouse. That's very typical for pre-retirees and baby boomers. As most of my clients have, Joe and Sally first attended my retirement education class at a local university. Instead of following the herd, they're willing to invest some time educating themselves to see if there's something else they need to be doing or learn more about a specific topic.

They learned that retirement is more than a stack of statements with a diversified pie chart and some magic number that needs to be saved. Joe and Sally realized that they wanted to take a more comprehensive approach to ensure that everything was being covered and working together in their best interest. The transition to retirement planning, and financial planning, imagine there's a wall full of light switches. If you flick one or two off, another two go on; you have to find that right combo for you.

By educating themselves on topics like Social Security and taxes in retirement, the order of withdrawals, and the transition from accumulation to distribution, they came to the conclusion that professional guidance would be needed. Joe and Sally needed someone in their corner, on an ongoing basis, to make sure they had that comprehensive plan in place.

Joe was 60, and Sally was 61 at the time. Their goal was to retire at 65 and 66 and feel comfortable and confident knowing that they have more than a stack of statements and a diversified portfolio. I call it a diversified pie chart and some magic number. As of today, they have drastically improved their tax efficiency for retirement income. They've planned out a well-thought Social Security strategy that gives them the most tax preferenced income for their retirement. Since they're married, that's important. That's in their best interest.

Now the savings they've been accumulating for 30 plus years are factored in for a time horizon when they're going to need that money for supplemental income in retirement. Joe and

Sally invested their time, and they didn't want to go about it the traditional way into their retirement planning. They went through the planning process, and now they have the peace of mind that they've always been searching for. It started by breaking down where they are now vs. where there wanted to go. Joe and Sally ran multiple scenarios and implemented those that added years of longevity to their savings and increased their after-tax income in retirement.

Your Homework Assignment

Your homework at the end of this chapter revolves around finding out the critical facts, uncovering all areas of comprehensive planning, and investing the time to make better decisions.

Topics such as Social Security and knowing why the most important factor is not when you take the benefit but how you take it; how tax planning for retirement is different than tax preparation. Can you right now map out a plan to lower your long-term tax bill but at the same time create more net income during your retirement years? What strategies or steps should be taken to defuse your tax-deferred accounts? Where should you draw income first in retirement, and at what amounts?

The bottom line is you do want to do your thorough education and invest some time to make sure you are going about it the comprehensive way, and you're not misguiding yourself, thinking that what you've been doing now will continue to work. It might continue to work, but if there are other ways of getting rid of some of your concerns and accomplishing your goals, the first step would be taking the time to get that education.

Chapter Two
The Perfect Storm

The Perfect Storm that baby boomers and pre-retirees face from my viewpoint is that different financial planning strategies may need to be used vs. retirees of the past. It's all about what's going on currently and some challenges that pre-retirees and baby boomers face. Unfunded promises to the American people. That's Social Security and Medicare, and if we're making decisions based upon what we're hearing or reading and not the facts and the math, we could make a decision maybe that's not in our best interest.

Inside the perfect storm, we also have record low-interest rates. The Federal Reserve has recently announced, and some expect to stay where they are now and low until 2023. A low-interest-rate environment could stay relatively low for some time.

The Perfect Storm

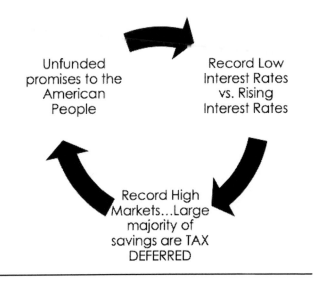

Unfunded promises to the American People

Record Low Interest Rates vs. Rising Interest Rates

Record High Markets...Large majority of savings are TAX DEFERRED

As the government borrowings increase dramatically, it can be very popular to keep these rates low. The fork in the road comes in because borrowers love these low rates, but it presents retirees with some investment challenges. We've never been here before all at once. Interest rates, since the late eighties, have been declining. Now we're at a point where they're so low, we can either go to a negative interest rate, or the rates could start creeping up, increasing. How's that going to affect your retirement?

We cannot forget this thing called inflation either. The combination of low-interest rates and higher inflation may force some retirees to take on more market risk than normal. This mentality of being more conservative as you approach or go through your retirement years might just be the downfall of your investment longevity.

Then we throw in market risk plus record-high market volatility. One of the risks to be wary of is the sequence of returns risk. Pre-retirees and those recently retired can expose themselves to being forced to sell at losses early because of too much market risk. The nest egg could experience a downward swing in value while drawing out income. No one has a crystal ball, so this is nothing really other than unlucky timing for most. The end result is your nest egg often cannot fully recover even when the markets bounce back. Primarily due to the regular withdrawals vs. regular contributions one is used to. Uncertainty is the new norm for baby boomers when it comes to the markets. No one could have predicted the pandemic or where the market would be now or even in 5 years from now. The most valuable asset to investing is time, and while younger investors, just as you once did, can ride out periods of volatility. Retirees and pre-retirees may need to rethink their retirement investment strategy.

What "Is" and "Isn't" in Your Control

Most individuals or couples think that they don't have any control of their taxes or investment performance, but they do. The decisions you're making now give you control over the future changes and opportunities as they arise. If taxes go up at some point, have you made decisions already where that won't affect you? There are a lot of little things like that. You do have more control than you would think you do. You can't control the stock market and what laws and bills and legislations pass, but you can make decisions and put strategies in place to be better prepared for when it does happen. The tax book says, "Here's what you legally can and can't do." There are things that you do have control of, though.

Planning comprehensively, you're making decisions, not looking at your investments alone. Again, most pre-retirees and baby boomers have their stack of statements or are only focused on the investment piece. As many pre-retirees do, maybe you are working with a financial advisor disguised as a broker. He or she is focused on gathering assets and sales. A majority of the industry is set up to only focus on some type of particular product or selling a certain type of investment. Your retirement plan should be bigger than just some stocks, mutual funds, and a pie chart. Pulling out some magical withdrawal rate and then riding out markets. A well-designed retirement plan could allow you to have better control on your NET income, and get an extra $10,000 of Social Security Tax-free each year, and possibly save you hundreds of thousands of dollars in taxes. Have a plan laid out on what you're trying to accomplish short and long term. Not just on your investments but also from an income and tax perspective. That way, when stuff does happen, you've already controlled the narrative on it instead of reacting emotionally. It is more likely if you are working with a financial advisor disguised as a broker, you will hear, "don't worry, the stock market has never failed to recover" or "we do not give any tax advice, but you can consult with your tax professional."

Taxes will go up, and taxes will go down, historically. The stock market will crash up, and it will crash down, but the impact on your accounts will be different in accumulation vs. distribution. I don't have a crystal ball. Neither do you or your broker. Going against what logic or math might suggest is in your best interest, a large majority of pre-retirees and baby boomers will continue down the path of traditional retirement planning by continuing to save away in tax-deferred accounts and then show income in retirement out of these same accounts year after year in retirement. Why would this be the case? Change is often hard when it comes to your finances, and sometimes one must go against conventional wisdom to accomplish their goal. "Keep saving and deferring they said. Don't worry because when you retire, you'll be in a lower tax bracket." That could be true for some, but most pre-retirees would agree tax rates will go up in the future for most people. Those same people who agreed that tax hikes are likely in the future are the same ones who haven't done anything about it. Making assumptions about retirement without running the numbers and looking at the math is a very common mistake.

Lesson Two
Comprehensive Approach

Chapter Three
Income Plan

Any income plan should typically include:

- Social Security Maximization

- Cash Flow or Expense Analysis

- Order Of Withdrawals In Retirement

- Inflation

The first step to building a retirement plan in your best interest is to focus on your income plan. You save away in your TAXED LATER Accounts while you work 20, 30, 40 years. You're saving all this money somewhere in return for it to pay you an income. You are hoping you have saved enough to supplement the income needed in addition to maybe your Social Security or a pension. As any pre-retiree should remain long-term-minded, the supplemental income from investments and other sources needs to last as long as you do.

For some, this means, have you accumulated enough to last you 30 plus years.

An easy place to start is by looking at the net deposits on a monthly basis from your paycheck. What is the net amount of income needed to replace what you are currently living off of right now? It is very common for pre-retirees to want to maintain their current lifestyle, but if you are looking to increase lifestyle, then that must be factored in also. Most individuals don't even know what that number needs to be. I often hear some random annual or monthly income number desired to live off of in retirement, but this is often a guess. You only get one shot at retirement, so why not do a little homework. T

There are unknown variables. How long are you going to live? How long are you going to need your money to last? That's one of the top concerns: "Will I run out of money?" A good starting point could be to do a test run the year prior to retirement. Another option is to run a current cash flow analysis or an income and expense, or a budget, whatever you want to call it. What are you living on right now? Modern banking makes this process super simple to find and track.

In retirement, are you trying to maintain your lifestyle? Are you going to live on less? What are you going to do? Will the cost of your medical coverage go up or down? This mainly depends on the Medicare coverage you elect, or if you are retiring prior to 65 then taking on COBRA or private insurance. This gives you a starting point of how much you're going to need monthly in retirement. After you gain a better understanding of the NET income you're going to need, then it's time to take a look at the income sources that could be paying you in retirement.

Year Born	Full Retirement Age (FRA) 100% Benefit
1937	65
1938	65 and 2 months
1939	65 and 4 months
1940	65 and 6 months
1941	65 and 8 months
1942	65 and 10 months
1943 to 1954	66
1955	66 and 2 months
1956	66 and 4 months
1957	66 and 6 months
1958	66 and 8 months
1959	66 and 10 months
1960 and later	67

FRA – Full Retirement Age

- The age in which individuals become eligible to receive full/unreduced benefits is called the FRA (Full Retirement Age) -- or Normal Retirement Age.

- Benefits can begin as early as age 62 and as late as age 70.

https://www.socialsecurity.gov/planners/retire/agereduction.html

Since Social Security is an entitlement program, let's focus on that. Everybody should agree that Social Security is part of your income plan. However, baby boomers vastly underestimate the impact it has on your overall retirement. It plays a major role in your taxes in retirement, but also the withdrawal rate from your retirement portfolio. My goal in this section of the book is the teach you how to avoid the critical mistakes I see so many baby boomers make when claiming their Social Security. The first thing you need to do is put together a Social Security maximization plan, but before getting started, let's look at what you need to know.

1. Understand the order of withdrawals

2. Not all money and income is taxed the same

3. Maximizing your Social Security is about how not when

Can you say right now how you are truly going to maximize Social Security around your retirement assets? This is going to take some education where it's not about when you take your Social Security. It's about how you take it. Social Security maximization is not just waiting until age 70 to take claim a benefit because, on paper, it's a higher amount.

Question:

Mathematically, do you know when it's in your best interest to file for your Social Security?

Doesn't it make more sense to take an earlier benefit at 62 and get paid for a longer amount of time than waiting until age 70?

From my experience, it is a very common and costly mistake to take benefits before or at Full Retirement Age. This mainly pertains to those households where a majority of their savings and income will come from tax-deferred accounts. The ultimate factor is the size of those tax-deferred accounts, the percentage of the make-up of the tax-deferred accounts of the household's total assets, and lastly, the income needed or desired in retirement. Again, this is not true for every case. Before you even consider implementing any strategy, please consult with a professional advisor.

Chapter Four
Putting It All Together

1. Breakeven points are something to consider when it comes to different claiming ages, but it should not be the overwhelming factor. Unless you have a crystal ball on the future and how long it will be until you are called up or down.

2. Spousal Consideration can play a critical role in when and how you claim. The tricky element is most pre-retirees are stuck in the now, and how does it work if I take it now. Later on, in the book, you will learn more about how taxes will ultimately play the largest role on when you may claim, but for now, understand if you are married and one spouse passes, the higher of the two payments will continue. The lower of the two payments then goes away. It is very common for the higher income earner to delay, but again do not make basic assumptions.

Consider what it would look like for the survivor in 20 years if benefits were claimed at 62. Then compare that to what the survivor would receive if claimed at Full Retirement or even 70. Most times, when this type of consideration is made, it an increase between 43-93% more for the survivor.

3. Tax advantages of Social Security vs. Tax-Deferred Accounts withdrawals

Pop Quiz: If you take $1000 from a Traditional IRA or 401k or get $1000 from Social Security, which is worth more?

Answer: Social Security! 15% is always Tax-Free

4. Where are you now? If a large majority of your retirement assets are in TAXED LATER accounts such as 401k's and IRA's, then you must understand the order of withdrawals.

Scenario

1. It could possibly be in your best interest to use your TAXED LATER accounts first and delay claiming until later.

2. Delayed Credits on your payments would then compound, plus any COLA increases. After your Full Retirement Age, this would be 8% plus COLA.

3. Couple your household Social Security income and withdrawals from Tax-Free accounts at age 70 or claiming age desired.

4. Most importantly, by taking a comprehensive approach, you now factor in that not all money and income are taxed the same.

Traditional Income Plan

Social Security = $70,000

IRA Withdrawals = $50,000

Annual Income = $120,000

12% Marginal Rate

Estimated Federal Tax = $7,219

$40,850 of the Social Security Taxable @ 12%

Retire Ready Income Plan

Social Security = $70,000

IRA Withdrawals = $15,000

ROTH IRA Withdrawals = $30,000

Annual Income = $115,000

0% Marginal Rate

Estimated Federal Tax = $0

$10,845 of the Social Security Taxable @ 0%

What will it take for you to get the net income you desire? Social Security, in and of itself, is not taxable, but other sources of income that come in from your retirement could and will determine the taxable amount of your Social Security. It depends on what you have saved or what other income you have, whether it is in the form of pensions, dividends, or IRA withdrawals. Certain types of resources like that can cause your Social Security to be worth less than you originally thought.

The determining factor in whether or not you will have to pay taxes on your Social Security is called the Provisional Income Calculation. If you're single or you're married, there are different priorities, but again, you want to get to the point where you're maximizing that income benefit.

Inside your income plan, you're going to put together a comparison of two to three different orders of withdrawals. Maybe the first one consists of taking Social Security upon retirement plus supplementing income with the use of Tax-Deferred accounts. The next can look at the possibility of delaying Social

Security and withdrawing first from those IRA's and 401k's. Once you understand the order of money and how Social Security is deemed taxable (Provisional Income Calculation), then you are also executing a ROTH Conversion strategy during this timeframe. What amounts and from what accounts are you going to spend first and in combination with or without Social Security? If you are looking at retirement comprehensively, forward-looking tax ideas could ultimately determine where you draw from first. With Social Security, math might suggest showing as little IRA withdrawals and taxable dividends as possible to maximize that income. The more income you show as ordinary income, which could be IRA withdrawals or pensions, could make your Social Security more taxable. The end result is then taking a larger monthly withdrawal from your nest egg.

Inflation is also important. Inflation's a big deal. If you laid out your cash flow plan and said, "We're going to need $80,000 after tax to live the retirement we want," in five or ten years, you're going to need more than $80,000. Using the rule of 72, if you assume a 4%

inflation, then you will actually need $160,000 net in 18 years. Keep in mind that whatever you have saved in your nest egg, you're going to need a little more of that every year as you retire. It's very important to properly factor in inflation when you consider the income you will need for your expenses during the course of retirement. Social Security, for the time, is being inflation-adjusted, so getting this correct is very important. Unless you have a trust fund sitting somewhere, this is the biggest decision for most baby boomers. It affects the amount of income collected over, the amount of total taxes that will be paid, the withdrawal rate needed from retirement accounts, and then the final balance left for spouse or beneficiaries.

Chapter Five
Grab a Pencil and Paper

Let's consider a husband and wife who are both full-time employees. The first thing you want to do is get out your pay stub and go to your net pay. How much net pay is going into your bank account every two weeks or every month?

Let's say net pay for both household members is 6,500 bucks a month. That tells them $6,500 bucks a month is coming into their bank account, which they are using to live on. From there, go into your budget and break down, of the 6,500 a month, how much of that are you truly using to live? Where is the cash flow of this money going? That's going to help you narrow down the number you're going to need for retirement.

Again, that goes back to whether you are trying to maintain your lifestyle in retirement or increase for the go-go years. Are there some expenses eating up some of that $6,500 that will go away? Maybe a mortgage will be paid off by then, or your health insurance or whatever else. Those are those little X factors to keep in mind. What you are living on right now from your paychecks is a pretty good starting point.

Remember, priority number one is figuring out how much income your investments truly need to pay you and what is the best order of withdrawals to achieve this in your best interest. Once a pre-retiree can get math and compounding on his or her side, then making investment and tax planning decisions should follow. The entire point of accumulation is to get your retirement assets to pay you income. Why not get every single nickel and dime from your Social Security benefit? Why not begin to plan on the order of withdrawals to make your income in retirement as efficient as possible?

THE SMART TAX
ROADMAP
"NOT ALL INCOME IS TAXED THE SAME"

Case Study

Traditional "Conventional Wisdom" Order of Withdrawals

1. $2,000,000 Taxed Later "IRA's and 401k's."

2. Combined Social Security of $60,000 @ Full Retirement Age

3. Order of Withdrawals

    a. Social Security + Taxed Later

4. Annual Gross Income of $130,000

5. 22% Federal Marginal Rate

6. Estimated $11,143 Federal Taxes

7. $51,000 of Social Security benefits taxable at 22%

What if I told you there could be a strategy that could reduce the long-term tax bill in retirement and possibly even get it down to zero?

Let's get started!

Case Study

Forward Looking

1. $2,000,000 Taxed Later "IRA's and 401k's"

2. Combined Social Security of $74,000 @ 70

3. Order of Withdrawals

    a. Taxed Later + Conversions

    b. Social Security + Taxed Later + ROTH IRA

4. Upfront Taxes Paid so @ 70

    a. Social Security: $74,000

Taxed Later Income: $15,000

ROTH IRA Income: $40,000

5. 10% Federal Marginal Rate

6. Estimated $0 Federal Taxes

7. $13,225 of Social Security benefits taxable at 10%

8. $15,000 + $13,225 = $28,225 Taxable Income

9. Standard Deduction of $29,336

$0 Taxes Due

Lesson Three:
The Smart Tax Road Map

Chapter Six
Taxes In Retirement

Any comprehensive retirement plan will include strategies for decreasing tax liabilities now and later. This typically includes:

- Assessing the taxable nature of your current holdings

- Pay now vs. Pay Later

- Strategizing ways to include tax-deferred or tax-free money in your plan

- Strategize which tax funnel to draw income from first to potentially reduce the tax burden.

This step is typically the most overlooked planning aspect for pre-retirees when it comes to retirement planning. The main focus is typically stock picking or market timing for most pre-retirees, but the comprehensive approach knows the value of SMART tax planning. Typically, we become glorified tax filers during our working year, and whomever we're working with is a tax filer. A good place to start is to know the difference between tax preparation vs. tax planning. Tax Planning is the analysis of a financial situation or plan from a tax perspective. The purpose of tax planning is to ensure tax efficiency. The Federal income tax bill for a majority of pre-retirees will be their largest retirement expense.

I believe you should begin the process by first completing a self-examination or MRI of where you are at now.

Tax Forward True/False Quiz

1. I know what order my accounts should be used in retirement to achieve tax efficiency.

2. I feel that every year I've explored all available techniques to benefit my situation.

3. I have a clearly written, forward-looking, tax-efficient plan to accomplish my short-term and long-term goals.

4. I understand how the taxation system works for my brokerage accounts, tax-deferred accounts, Social Security, and how I can use these systems to my full advantage.

5. I know how to "Maximize" my Social Security around my retirement accounts.

A majority of the industry is only focused on gathering assets and giving you a diversified pie chart, but your retirement should be much bigger than that. Most folks have saved for 20, 30, and maybe even 40 years for their nest egg. Hence why right now, you are probably sitting there with a stack of statements, a diversified pie chart, and a Social Security statement.

True alpha comes in the form of ongoing comprehensive or comprehensive planning. How can you create extra wealth or net income with the retirement assets you have right now. Are there decisions to be made to begin shifting to different tax funnels, so you can then spend those lifelong savings efficiently? For some of you, the answer might be no, but for many of you, the answer is yes. As a fiduciary advisor who takes a comprehensive approach, I am looking at the present but also looking towards the future.

The best way to walk through this process is what I call THE SMART TAX ROADMAP "NOT ALL INCOME IS TAXED THE SAME."

STOP 1: Master Provisional Income

Provisional Income			
Non-Taxable Interest	Ordinary Income	Dividends and Capital Gains	50% of Social Security Benefit

Provisional Income
The determining factor in whether you will have to pay taxes on your Social Security benefits.

The Provisional Income calculation is used by the IRS to determine how much of your household benefit will be taxable. It is calculated by adding up the recipient's gross ordinary income, tax-free interest, dividends, or capital gains, and then 50% of the Social Security benefit.

Once you get the sum of the Provisional Income calculation, you know now how much of your benefits could or will be taxable.

Filing Status	Provisional Income	Amount of Social Security benefits subject to tax
Married filing jointly	Under $32,000 $32,000 to $44,000 Over $44,000	0% 50% 85%
Single, head of household, widow, widower, married filing separately and living apart from spouse	Under $25,000 $25,000 to $34,000 Over $34,000	0% 50% 85%
Married filing separately and living with spouse	Over $0	85%

For the 2021 tax year, 15% of all Social Security benefits remain tax-free. Please note that Social Security in and of itself is not taxable, but other sources of income can cause it to be taxable.

You don't pay taxes on any of your Social Security benefits if:

- You're filing as an individual and have a provisional income of less than $25,000

- You're filing a joint return and have a provisional income of less than $32,000

You may have to pay income tax on up to 50% of your Social Security benefits if:

- You're filing as an individual, and you have provisional income between $25,000 and $34,000

- You're filing a joint return and have provisional income between $32,000 and $44,000

You may have to pay income tax on up to 85% of your Social Security benefits if:

- You're filing as an individual, and you have a provisional income of more than $34,000

- You're filing a joint return and have a provisional income of more than $44,000

STOP 2: Categorize Money by Tax Impact

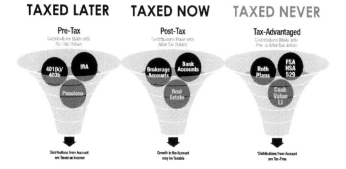

TAXED LATER   **TAXED NOW**   TAXED NEVER

The first thing you need to do is categorize your money or accounts by tax impact. You're going to have three funnels, and remember these funnels because, eventually, we're going to use these funnels to fill up your buckets later in the book. This is a critical step to confirming your Order Of Withdrawals is set up by what the math says to do.

The first funnel is TAXED LATER. This is your pre-tax money, which consists of contributions made with pre-tax dollars. Most popular is your 401(k), your 403(b)s, your IRAs, or maybe even your pension. When you take distributions from this funnel, from this account, you are taxed at ordinary income. Keep in mind anything that's pulled from this funnel can make your Social Security more

taxable "TAXED AS ORDINARY INCOME".
It would be very common if today, 100% of
your retirement accounts are held in this funnel,
banking on the notion that when you retire, you
will be in a lower tax bracket for the next 30
years.

The second funnel is TAXED NOW. This
would consist of post-tax savings. Here,
contributions are made with after-tax dollars.
Growth in the account may or may not be
taxable. This would include brokerage accounts,
banks accounts, and real estate. Depending on
how it's executed, it's either going to be a short-
term gain taxed as ordinary income or a long-
term gain taxed at long-term capital gains rates.
Keep in mind any income or distribution shown
for the current tax year from this can make your
Social Security more taxable. It is part of the
provisional income calculation.

The third funnel is the least popular when it
comes to percentages. This is the TAXED
NEVER funnel. Contributions are made with
pre-after-tax dollars. Since 99% of households I
meet regularly are heavy on the TAXED
LATER funnel, it is typically too late to make

enough contributions here to have a major impact. The major solution to the problem could instead come in the form of ROTH conversions.

Distributions from the account are tax-free. The key is you've paid the tax, the growth is tax-free, and then distribution from the account in retirement is tax-free. We talked about that perfect storm. You've already paid your taxes upfront. If rising taxes happen in 10 years, for example, it doesn't affect you in this funnel. If markets are experiencing unfavorable returns for a couple of months or years, then you can lean on the ROTH for income. You do not need to liquidate as many or shares or sell as big of a loss since you do not need to withhold state and federal taxes.

The biggest bonus of this funnel is it does not cause your Social Security to become more taxable. It allows you to keep more of your Social Security and potentially lower the withdrawal on your retirement accounts.

STOP 3: Understand the Order of Withdrawals

One of the obstacles pre-retirees face in Step 2 is strategizing the most advantageous way to draw from savings while minimizing taxes. After Step 1, if you are heavily weighted in the TAX LATER funnel, you still have a window of opportunity to tax advantage of the Tax Cuts and Jobs Act. In some instances, households have already done a great job at saving inside the TAXED NOW and TAXED LATER but still need to map out the order of withdrawals around other sources of income.

Everyone has different priorities, goals, and concerns in retirement. At the top of the list usually falls outliving those retirement assets. "Do we have enough" is something I often hear during Discovery with a household. I always reply that a tax-efficient withdrawal strategy can extend the life of your portfolio, and at the same time, increase your spending power during retirement.

Chapter Seven
Case Study

Scenario 1

Here we are going to take a household with a very modest income. In this type of scenario, we are going to take advantage of income that is subject to very low tax rates. To make it simple, consider using or filling up the brackets with ordinary income from those TAXED LATER accounts first. This would mean distributions or withdrawals from something like a Traditional IRA or 401k. Take advantage of the massive standard deduction, 10 and 12% brackets with these withdrawals. The TCJA has created this single greatest opportunity in most baby boomer's lifetime. Massive opportunity to either start paying or reducing those taxes in retirement, even if you are still working and have years before retirement. However, depending on the size of your TAXED LATER funnel and desired NET INCOME, you could find yourself sitting on a massive tax trap in the future. You may end up trying to keep the tax bill low or, for example, at the 12% rate, but eventually forced in a higher tax rate that remainder years. This could cause your Social Security and investments to be all hit with a higher marginal rate. Be cautious that if you are going to spend TAX LATER accounts first and delay Social Security to consider adding ROTH Conversions. This could be one step closer to getting tax-advantaged income for the rest of your life.

Scenario 2

If you do not currently have brokerage accounts with capital gains, you can skip this section of the book.

In this scenario, we are going to harvest those untaxed capital gains. If your taxable income is less than $40,400 (Single) or $80,800 (Joint), long-term capital gains or qualified dividends are not taxed. Please keep in mind everything I am discussing is based on the TCJA and current law, but the massive standard deduction is very beneficial here.

For example, let's take a look at a married couple who has $2,000,000 saved for retirement. Based on their funnels, 50% TAX Later, 40% TAXED NOW, and then 10% TAXED NEVER. The household will bring in $45,000 from Social Security and will spend $120,000 per year. After going through the tax planning process, it was determined best to spend the taxable accounts prior to RMD's. After, a combination of withdrawals from taxable, ROTH, and RMD's. This was deemed in their best interest because the married couple could avoid capital gains taxes until the ROTH account was depleted.

Understanding and maximizing your own custom order of withdrawals can add years to the longevity of your portfolio. Another factor of this step is lowering your overall tax bill during retirement.

STOP 4: Measure Your Tax Bracket Capacity

Look at your retirement tax plan as a measuring cup. First, you are going to need your most recent federal tax return! Identify where you are now and then where you want to go. Do you currently have excess room inside of your current marginal rate?

The main takeaway from this step would be to seek out tax planning opportunities

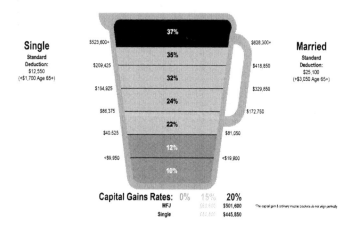

Case Study Scenario

A 64-year-old married couple retires early, for what that means is up to you. They have done the math and believe it is in their best interest to delay Social Security until 70. This decision came to fruition by going through a comprehensive planning process. The decision was not made by looking at their statement and seeing they collect a higher payment the longer they waited. It was in their best interest to delay Social Security, realize Capital Gains in a fresh tax year, then implement a tax strategy to move enough savings from TAXED LATER to TAXED NEVER. The ROTH Conversions were done while delaying Social Security and after capital gains were realized.

Their brokerage account held roughly $350,000 with a $260,000 basis. Combined, the couple also held around $500,000 in TAXED LATER Accounts. They had no savings upon retirement in the TAXED NEVER funnel. This was a big concern for the couple. At age 64, with no other income to be shown, they sell off their brokerage account. This triggers a $90,000 long-term capital gain event for the year. The measuring cup was optimized for the given year but also for every year moving forward. From ages 65-70, they planned on living off the brokerage account tax-free. During these years, they started ROTH Conversions up to the 12% bracket. At age 70, the married couple then claimed their Social Security benefits. This custom planning now allowed their Social Security to be tax-free, locked into the lowest tier Medicare premium, RMD's would not force them into a higher bracket or cause more of their Social Security to be more taxable. Lastly, in insured the surviving spouse would bracket jump upon death.

STOP 5: Pay Now vs. Pay Later

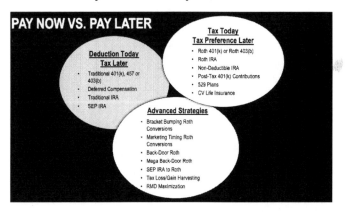

Remember, retirement isn't just about saving enough money to last a lifetime. It needs to also be about keeping as much of retirement accounts as possible and spending those savings in a tax-efficient manner. The end goal for everyone is maximizing net income. Disguised financial advisors talk a lot about market risks, longevity, etc. Reducing your taxes over your retirement should be close to the top, if not at the top. Not doing anything at all could be the biggest challenge facing baby boomers, with everything saved away in the TAXED LATER funnel.

Almost every baby boomer would agree tax rates will go up at some point. What if a 50% increase came along during the first ten years of retirement. By the way, the math says they need to double, but let's pretend in the near future they go up 50%. The impact of this on those TAXED LATER accounts would be instrumental. You have a minority shareholder on those accounts with a majority vote. The minority shareholders know, at some point, you will be forced to withdraw from the pool of money not yet taxed. The SECURE ACT was recently passed on how your beneficiaries will now be taxed on these accounts too. Do yourself a favor and google the SECURE ACT and see those most recent updates. The first step is Uncle Sam starting to collect a larger piece of the pie.

Look at it from this viewpoint, you started a business where the contract states you get to keep 80% of the profits, and the silent partner gets to keep 20%. That seems like a great business model! However, built into the contract was a clause where your partner could come back and change the spilt to get a larger share. Maybe the partner over the years got him or herself into some major debt, so he or she comes back and now wants 30% of the profits, not 20%. Then after a few more years, the silent partner increases to a 60/40 split. This arrangement is what a vast majority of baby boomers are signed up for. A long time ago, you signed up for that 401k and made the decision to pay the tax on the harvest instead of the seed. The arrangement deal on your IRA's and 40lk's are with the government, and they really have control of how much they can take now and in the future. I look at it as a lifeline for cash flow if that need arises in the future.

You, in the end, decide how to pay the tax bill. I am in no way suggesting avoiding taxes, or you do not have to pay them. Tax planning is a process and can be complicated. Ask yourself this, if you knew your nest egg would drop 25% over the next month, would you do anything about it? I am assuming you would do something about that! If a large majority of your nest egg is in that TAX LATER funnel, then it may already be worth 25% less than the value given the IRA lien.

Go through a process and see whether or not it makes sense to implement strategy now, later, or not at all. Making assumptions can be your own downfall. Should you take advantage of present tax rates, probably the lowest in your lifetime, or continue kicking the tire down the tax road and hope our government suddenly adopts a habit of low taxes and low spending.

Chapter Eight
Who Should Engage In Tax Planning

1. Those who are thinking taxes will be higher in the future

2. Those who have excess room in the brackets

3. Those concerned about legacy planning for their surviving spouse

4. Those you have a majority of savings in TAXED LATER

5. Those who want to Maximize Social Security

The main goal in retirement tax planning is to plot out a roadmap to gain extra NET INCOME on a monthly basis. For some, it will take 10 years of strategies to get where you want to go. For others, it could be 4-5 years. My advice is to never just wing it, or fund some type of account, or "try" a ROTH conversion without any type of end goal.

A very common end goal for those who have roughly $500,000 to $3,000,000 in TAXED LATER accounts could be this:

1. Withdrawals from TAXED LATER accounts will be less than tax deductions and exemptions – TAX-FREE

2. Develop a strategy or plan to get enough annual income from Roth. – TAX-FREE

3. Social Security benefits at some point become TAX-FREE.

If you are making assumptions that you will pay less taxes in retirement, ignore taxes altogether, don't plan for Social Security taxation, and take withdrawals from retirement accounts in the wrong order, you could very well overpay your fair share.

"There are two systems of taxation in our country: one for the informed and one for the uninformed."
Learned Hand, Judge, United States Court of Appeals for the Second Circuit

STOP 6: Spousal Consideration

1. If you are married and one spouse dies, the surviving spouse is now *forced* (assuming they are 72) to take increasingly higher distributions as they age and will be taxed at single filer rates, which are much higher

2. Delaying the higher income earners Social Security Benefit will allow the surviving spouse a higher payment later in life

3. Consider using Tax-Deferred money to purchase Life Insurance or other tax planning strategies

Example for John and Sally

Scenario 1: both living

John Hopeful 81 & Sally Hopeful 75: Income needed $102,000 NET

Married over 65

1. John's Social Security: $45,000

2. Sally's Social Security: $30,000

3. Total IRA Distributions: $30,000

Federal Tax Due: $3,034 (12%)

Scenario 2: Lack of Spousal Consideration

Sally Hopeful (75): Income needed 92,000 NET

Single over 65

1. John's Social Security: $45,000

2. IRA Distributions: $47,000

Federal Tax Due: $10,780 (22%)

End Result of No Spousal Planning

1. Bracket Bumps for Sally

2. Only NET $81,220 for Sally

3. Effective Tax on next $1,000 from IRA = 41%

$34,675 Social Security Taxable

Lesson Four
How to Invest Without A
Crystal Ball

Chapter Nine
Investment Plan

As mentioned, many baby boomers and pre-retirees make this their first and only priority. Why are the disguised advisors only focused on your investments and having that stack of statements with a diversified pie chart?

Here is what I have seen. Number one, most people I meet, when I asked them why they're investing the way that they are, I find that they have trouble given me really clear-cut definitive answers.

They really don't know why they've got this percent in this fund or that percent in that fund, no, they're really not sure, and number two, they're really not sure if they're going to have enough money to retire. Will they outlive their retirement? They just don't know. As a result, you put those two things together, and it's no wonder why. We have so many sleepless nights.

That alone is what I call naked investing. Maybe you're picking funds with the best returns, but it doesn't apply to your income and tax plan. The decision alone is based on the historical average rate of return, but that is not the true CAGR "Compounded Annual Growth Return".

The Perfect Investment...

What would the perfect investment look like?

1. Never lose gains

2. Guarantee income for life

3. 100% liquidity

4. Double digits returns

5. Tax Efficient

This is what I call the Looney Tune Fund. The Looney Tune Fund is about as unrealistic as it gets. I hear these types of wants regularly, but this doesn't exist. No one investment can give you all of this. Every investment really has two of these three features. The three features are LIQUIDITY, PROTECTION, AND

GROWTH. For example, if you want PROTECTION AND LIQUIDITY, you know where to go. This would be your local bank or credit union. You get those two features and then give up the growth. You might just go broke safely in those CERTIFICATES OF DISSAPOINTMENT AT THE BANK. If you demand PROTECTION AND GROWTH, well, your option is Insurance of some type. The protection I am referencing is on a guaranteed basis of your principal. So, either the bank or the state backed. Please understand this, not all retirement insurance products are "protected" or have guaranteed principal protection. Finally, if you insist on wanting GROWTH AND LIQUIDITY, then you are 100% stock market-related. What are you willing to give up? The perfect investment doesn't exist!

How to Invest for Retirement Without a Crystal Ball

In THE SMART TAX ROADMAP, your tax funnels should have been completed. The next exercise of the comprehensive planning journey is to build an investment plan in your best interest. Now that you have the order of withdrawals, Social Security Maximization, and Taxes In Retirement Plan ready, you can make better-informed decisions on your nest egg. There is no best investing strategy. Everyone's financial situation is different. The moving parts that control the customized plan should be your income, risk tolerance, time horizon "when you need the money", current assets, and short and long-term financial goals. On top of all that, the Order of Withdrawals and Tax Plan should provide clarity and simplicity to making the investment allocations.

The 3 Secrets

1. Stocks cannot be skillfully picked

2. No one knows what the markets will do before they actually do it.

3. You are probably your own worst enemy.

"I'd compare stock pickers to astrologers, but I don't want to bad mouth astrologers."

Eugene Fama
American Economist

Lesson 1

Keep investing costs low! A sound investment plan can do this by utilizing individual stocks, low-cost index, and exchange-traded funds (ETF's).

Lesson 2

Do you remember this formula from high school algebra?

If $A > B$, and $B > C$, then $A > C$

Do you agree that the news is unpredictable? Do you agree the investment markets react to the news? Well, if the news is unpredictable then, the investment markets react.

"Experts" who got it wrong

"Dow could crash to 3,000 in 2013." --Harry Dent, Economist, Author of <u>The Great Depression Ahead</u>

"If Trump wins, you will see a market crash of epic proportions." --Steven Rattner, Economic Advisor to President Obama

"Mr. Obama is a disaster for business and a disaster for the United States." In the nine months following the interview, the S&P 500 had shot up by 20 percent. --Marc Faber, Economist

The financial media and investing "experts" can be our own worst enemy. The end result usually leads to buying high and selling low! In the accumulation phase, you are rewarded decades of time for overcoming this. The retirement phase of decumulation does not award you this time to "wait it out."

Lesson 3

When you start drawing out income from your portfolio, consistency of return is just as important as CAGR. Investing the nest egg based upon the time horizon of income or when you need the money can possibly give you that consistency.

The Stock Market Has Never Failed To Recover

The math of the investment plan long-term comes in the form of consistency of return vs. average return. There are a lot of ways but first, look at the most recent bear market other than now - the 2008 financial crisis. If you or your PLAN can't stomach the loss, then you shouldn't be in that investment. Look at the Standard deviation (be prepared for a little financial jargon).

It is the measurement of the volatility of the fund or total portfolio over time. Don't forget, markets are never consistent, but that's exactly what we want.

For example, maybe your disguised financial advisor of 20 years or your 401k states that you are averaging 8% over the last 10 years. Some disguised advisors, or quite possibly you, do a good job at growing your nest egg over time. We all know markets have always gone up over time, and if you are making frequent contributions to buy low and high, it helps increase that return. That same portfolio that has an average return of 8% also carries a standard deviation of 10. A pre-retiree might be thinking, "Hey, my broker accounts or 401k has never failed to recover from one of those 40% drops." Assumption kicks in that if I can continue to average 8%, then I can withdraw at a 5% rate to get the $50,000 I need each year on top of my Social Security.

So what does this mean?

1. 68% of the time: You will have a one-year return between -2% & 18%.

2. 95% of the time: You will have a one-year return between -12% & 28%.

3. 99% of the time: You will have a one-year return between -22% & 38%.

The point here is do not chase returns! Probably run an analysis using the 99% deviation. If you had $100,000 in the S&P 500 from 2000-2010 (no contributions or withdrawals), then that $100,000 was worth $95,000 at the end of 2010. This is called the last decade. If you put $100,000 in the S&P from 2010-2020, then it was worth $298,660. Man, the stock markets have been great, Kyle! If you had $100,000 in the S&P in 2000 and held until 2020, that was now worth $284,490. So, to sum this up, long-term investing works. These stock markets historically always go up over time when you buy and hold. The results will 100% be different when selling monthly to get income. The real rate of return from 2000-2020 was 5.4%, and this came with the big ups and the big downs.

The New Math

When does a $(-30) + 43 = 0$?

A $100,000 ROTH IRA drops 30% in one year. Yes, the markets can and will do this. Pre-retirees and baby boomers have been blessed with record bull markets returns in the decade! The standard deviation on your current mix of accounts might even show there is a 99% in any given year you will experience a return anywhere between -40% to a +60%. So, don't be surprised or emotionally overwhelmed when either happens! The question is, can you financially afford the larger drops before or at the beginning of retirement. Unless you have a crystal ball, then you or no one else knows the exact sequence of returns within that deviation range.

The ROTH drops 30% over the year, so the account holder has $70,000. The next year the portfolio does 43%! Congratulations, then ROTH has averaged a 6.5% average rate of return! Wait, you still only have $100,000 and averaged 6.5%? This is the math of retirement! The game changes the day you start needing income from the nest egg. The lower the deviation, the less volatile your returns can be year to year.

A great tax planning opportunity presents itself with this type of market drop, so those with a retirement tax plan would have taken advantage of the 30% drop. Understanding that investing is a long-term game, all the crashing up would result in tax-free growth.

Sequence of Returns

The biggest risk pre-retirees face comes in the form of sequence of returns. The first ten years' sequence of returns is the most important. Throw away the crystal ball or whatever the last decade has sequenced. This is risk that if you experience market declines in the early years of retirement, paired with reoccurring withdrawals, you can either deplete nest earlier than anticipated. "I thought if I just diversify to a 60/40 mix and withdraw 4%, this would last me 30 years." True, if your sequence of returns in the first ten years are favorable and no major declines. "What if I shift to be more conservative to avoid major losses" Very rarely do old investment philosophies work in the 21st century due to the low-interest-rate environment and market volatility. Just because you hit some magical savings number of $1 million does not mean the game is over.

Case Study

Two investors with a $1 million nest egg have average returns of 7% over 25 years, and both withdrew $60,000 per year (adjusted for inflation after the first year).

Mrs. Smith: Had a few great years at the beginning of retirement but hit a bear market towards the end. Ending balance: **Over $1 million at age 90**

Mr. Miller: Hit a bear market going into retirement but enjoyed a smoother road thereafter.

Ending balance: **$0 (ran out of money at age 88)**

Source: BlackRock. This graphic looks at the effect the sequence of returns can have on your portfolio value over a long period of time. Other factors that may affect the longevity of assets include the investment mix, taxes, expenses related to investing, and the number of years of retirement funding (life expectancy). This is a hypothetical illustration. This illustration assumes a hypothetical initial portfolio balance of $1,000,000, annual withdrawals of $60,000 adjusted annually by 3% for inflation, and the hypothetical sequence of returns noted in the table. These figures are for illustrative purposes only and do not represent any particular investment, nor do they reflect any investment fees, expenses, or taxes. When you are withdrawing money from a portfolio, your results can be affected by the sequence of returns even when the average return remains the same due to the compounding effect on the annual account balances and annual withdrawals.

21st Century Investing

Pre-retirees need to navigate market volatility, taxes, interest rates, and increasing life expectancies can be challenging when planning for retirement.

Investing too safely, and you run the risk of losing purchasing power due to inflation; investing too aggressively can expose you to significant financial loss. Both scenarios can create the risk of you running out of money prematurely in retirement

The first thing you're going to want to do is to assess your risk and volatility capacity. What's the real risk that you can take on or the growth that applies to you? Most people want more growth than they can afford because it also comes with a risk attached. You have to understand what you need your nest egg to do. If you can't afford a -32% in the 2nd year of retirement, is it worth carry that risk?

The fact is, without a comprehensive plan, we do not really know what we need long-term for our money to return. All is well until it isn't, and then you could be forced into a situation to sell at a major loss or cut back NET INCOME for a few months or years to "recover".

KISS

Keep it simple, stupid! I mentioned at the beginning of the book who the reading is not for. If you are a day trader, market speculator, or stock picker, this is not for you! Most investment plans work best when kept simple rather than made complicated. Simplicity is your friend! Avoid unnecessary complications or getting into something you do not understand. This does not mean you should settle for cookie-cutter models or portfolios. Make the process of why your money is where it is easy. Know why you have your ROTH invested like it is. Know why your IRA is invested like it is.

Almost every baby boomer or pre-retiree I talk to comes to me with the "Not Quite" plan. The "Not Quite" plan consists of some or all of the following:

Diversified pie chart

1. Some equity to the bond mix to meet their risk tolerance… 60/40%

2. Random individual stocks

3. Proprietary Mutual Funds from a wirehouse

4. High Yield Bonds

5. A 4-5% withdrawal rate in their head

6. Still carry a sequence of return risk

7. I think I pay 1%, but I am not sure…

This is what I call a WAG "Wild A** Guess."

Chapter Ten
Here Come the Buckets to the Rescue

Managing your nest egg in retirement is like playing a game of tug-of-war against yourself. You are trying to pull reoccurring income out every month but looking to grow the nest egg to support future spending to offset inflation.

The bucket strategy helps pre-retirees and retirees manage this tug-of-war. Remember those funnels back in the tax section? You will now use those funnels to fill up more buckets. The bucket strategy will also act as a guide to make sure you are spending your nest egg in the correct manner you laid out in the Order Of Withdrawals. It also assists in helping your make better decisions. You know now what accounts, what amounts, and the time horizon for the money. Bucket strategies are nothing new. There are multiple ideas and strategies out there on bucketing.

3 Bucket Approach

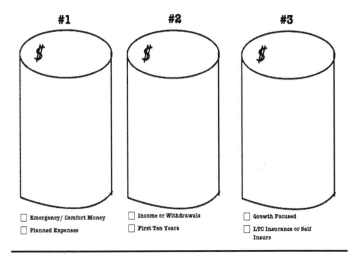

After two decades of declining interest rates and low yields, the traditional retirement of systematic withdrawals of 4% is facing challenges. To meet those challenges, I am going to apply a time horizon to the buckets. The concept is to invest based upon time horizon and purpose. The goal is to strategically position assets to plan for and mitigate the risks and dangers that can occur in retirement.

Where to consider before building the buckets out? You need to take into account your income needs, time horizon, and tax qualifications. Just like I have mentioned multiple times, everything in retirement planning should be customized to your personal situation. The bucket strategy is not telling you where to invest or what to invest in but bringing purpose and simplicity to the investment plan.

Bucket 1

If you go back to the three characteristics any investment can have, then this bucket is 100% giving up growth. The yields on cash in the bank or certificates of disappointment are close to zero. This bucket can be label as *SAFE or LIQUID.

*Money referred to as safe in Bucket 1 is intended to main money held in a bank and subject to FDIC limitations

Avoid rules of thumb when it comes to investing, but especially when it comes to what needs to be in the bank. Find that "sleep at night" number that needs to be in bucket 1. This includes emergency or planned expenses, plus on average 0-12 months of income.

Bucket 2

Remember, you can customize this strategy with as many buckets as you desire. You can customize what type of assets are held in the buckets, but this strategy is showing a 3 Bucket approach. The main difference is I am applying a time horizon to the buckets. Bucket 2 contains the first 10 years of your retirement income or living expenses. This is the most important bucket and the bucket most people do not have in place. Depending on the risk that you appropriated, this will typically be in less volatile investments and more conservative or income-focused stocks. At the end of the day, conservative or moderate means something different to everyone.

Why is the comprehensive planning approach so valuable? Everything is tied together and focuses on making decisions in your best interest. Better informed decisions lead to that desired retirement and allow you to sleep at night.

Go back to your income plan, where you put together the Social Security Maximization strategy. When are you taking Social Security?

If you're delaying your Social Security to do more tax of the tax planning "ROTH CONVERSION" or "CAPITAL GAINS HARVESTING", then you're going to have more of your savings in bucket 2 because you will lean on it more in the first ten years. You are doing this to spend tax-deferred or capital gains at a lower or zero rate, to get tax-advantaged income for the rest of your life.

Bucket 2 is the first phase of retirement income. The final number determined in total comes down to tax qualifications, inflation, and how you are claiming Social Security. If you decide to claim early or on time, you might need a lesser percentage of your nest egg in bucket 2. You will need more of your nest egg later in life to do the heavy lifting. Bucket 2 sole purpose is to avoid as much as possible the risk of being forced to sell during a downward swing. This ultimately causes you to liquidate a bigger piece of the overall portfolio for the same amount of income. If you implemented tax planning strategies, then you still need to sell more shares to pay Uncle Sam.

Potential Investment Choices

1. Structured Notes

2. Dividend Stocks or Dividend Funds

3. Bonds

4. Annuities

A pre-retiree goes from Dollar Cost Averaging to Reverse Dollar Cost Averaging. You will be forced to sell high and sell low in retirement. The impact of this comes in the sequence you experience during the first decade of retirement. The purpose is to insure against what can go wrong "Sequence Of Returns", to acquire the luxury of what can go right in the bucket.

The First 10 Years Are The Most Important

Steve $500,000
Retired in 1990

Bill $500,000
Retired in 2000

End of Year	Market Return[1]	Withdrawal	IRA Account Balance
1990	-4.34%	$ 30,000	$ 449,602
1991	20.32%	$ 30,000	$ 504,865
1992	4.17%	$ 30,000	$ 494,667
1993	13.72%	$ 30,000	$ 528,419
1994	2.14%	$ 30,000	$ 509,085
1995	33.45%	$ 30,000	$ 639,340
1996	26.01%	$ 30,000	$ 767,829
1997	22.64%	$ 30,000	$ 904,873
1998	16.10%	$ 30,000	$ 1,015,728
1999	25.22%	$ 30,000	$ 1,234,328

End of Year	Market Return[1]	Withdrawal	IRA Account Balance
2000	-6.18%	$ 30,000	$ 440,954
2001	-7.10%	$ 30,000	$ 381,776
2002	-16.76%	$ 30,000	$ 292,819
2003	25.32%	$ 30,000	$ 329,364
2004	3.15%	$ 30,000	$ 308,794
2005	-0.61%	$ 30,000	$ 277,094
2006	16.29%	$ 30,000	$ 287,345
2007	6.43%	$ 30,000	$ 273,892
2008	-33.84%	$ 30,000	$ 161,359
2009	18.82%	$ 30,000	$ 156,081

Bucket 3

The third bucket is the longest-term portion of your nest egg. Think about it like this. Let's say John is five years away from retirement. After going through a comprehensive process, he began to build out his bucket strategy. If he's five years away from retirement, anything that's invested in bucket 3, he's not going to need for 15 years. He has successfully broken down his nest egg into the time horizon. Typically, that's going to be growth-focused, long-term growth-focused.

The 3rd bucket's primary focus is growth. If he commits to the tax planning, then some Roth conversions might occur in the 3rd bucket. Another goal typically planned for in this bucket would be to self-insure for Long Term Care costs. If you know there is a portion of your nest egg that will not be needed for 10 plus years, it can bring clarity to the investment vehicles.

Maybe you're down 28% in a month. You can go to bed at night knowing that, as long as you stick to it and stay invested, it will come back over time. In the 3rd bucket, the key here is you have bought a time horizon where you can choose to invest in vehicles with a longer-term horizon commitment and greater growth potential with more confidence. This bucket is usually dominated by stocks and equities because this is likely to deliver the best long-term performance. At the same time, this portion of the nest egg will carry the greater loss potential. I

Traditionally you have the "not quite" plan. You have two buckets, bucket 1 and a diversified pie chart bucket. Bucket 1 is still your money in the bank, but your diversified pie chart is more of a WAG.

What's My Point

To sum it up, you must divide your savings into buckets based upon the needs and time horizon. Apply the proper time horizon to each bucket and invest accordingly. By doing so, you can help protect from the sequence of returns risk, I call it the red zone, in your first ten years of retirement. You have the money set there aside.

However, also keep this in mind: we have to be realistic. Determine your priorities and what you're willing to give up. There's no such thing as a perfect investment. Are you willing to give up liquidity to have protection and growth? Are you willing to give up protection to have liquidity and growth, or do you want to be all stock market-based? Maybe you want to have all your money in the bank, and you want no growth, but you want it to be liquid and protected. You have to find your priorities inside the buckets. As Warren Buffett says, "An idiot with a plan can beat a genius without a plan."

Bucket sizes vary with your needs and goals. For some, a larger portion might fall in bucket 2 because you will need the income sooner rather than later. For others, the 3rd bucket can be the largest of the buckets. How much time do you have before you need the money invested? What type of returns and standard deviation do you want? Are you near retirement?

My Encouragement to You

If you're at the point where you're looking for an advisor/client relationship, my advice would be to look for someone independent, fiduciary, fee-only, and he or she uses a comprehensive planning approach. The comprehensive advisor can show you from day one value and the ongoing value. Income strategies, order of withdrawals to increase your net income in retirement, tax strategies to lower your long-term tax bill to Uncle. They use smart and low-cost investing vehicles. Make sure that their experience and their recommendations are truly customized to you. If you are with a large broker or wirehouse, it is very likely you are stuck in a model or cookie-cutter program.

Also, you need to have a full understanding of the fee program. What are you paying for? Nine times out of 10, someone cannot tell me their fee structure. "I have been with my broker for 16 years, and I think I pay 1%. A fee analysis then shows a total cost of 2.3%. The fee structure should be simple.

Unlike many of the Wall Street brokerage firms, you may be familiar with, I do not layer in fees and expenses that are typical of the mutual funds that many brokerage firms utilize. I keep my client's expenses very low by utilizing individual stocks and low-cost index funds, and exchange-traded funds (ETF's) from providers such as Vanguard.

Many of the brokers or disguised advisors receive commissions, "kickbacks", 12b-1 fees, revenue-sharing fees, or any of the other forms of "back door" payments.

At the End of the Day

Just working with the fiduciary or advisor doesn't mean much. Going to some retirement education class or reading this book isn't enough. There are plenty of fiduciaries out there who do traditional retirement planning. Let me be very clear; not everyone needs professional help. It comes down to what you do now. If there was a missing piece of information that was costing you money now or could potentially cost you significantly more money in the future, when would you want to find out about it?

For many pre-retirees and retirees, the biggest reduction to your income could be from the decisions you do or do not make.

Self-Assessment

1. Do my current allocations plan for and mitigate market risk, interest rate risk, and sequence of returns risk?

2. Do my current retirement plans consider the best Order Of Withdrawals?

3. Do I have a 2nd bucket in place to meet my needs in the first phase stage of retirement?

4. Does my current plan proactively defuse tax time bombs?

Here's What It Takes to Financially Educate Yourself to Be Retirement Ready!

Congratulations! You're rounding the corner towards retirement, what you've always worked towards. You've done a great job saving and investing in your 401(k) and IRAs. Now it's time to start working towards getting the money out, so you can enjoy your retirement.

Wouldn't it be nice if there were someone to help you figure out how to best get the money out of your accounts like there was to get the money into those accounts? Even better is someone to talk to about doing it in the most beneficial way for you, not the government. When I say government, I mean only paying the necessary taxes instead of double taxes.

Once pre-retirees can be confident, comfortable and start taking control of their retirement planning, it allows them to become *Retire Ready*.

My hope is that after reading this book, you are inspired to become Retirement Ready.